CREATIVE ACTIVITIES
FOR
BEGINNING
READERS

Written and illustrated by Sandy Baker

Good Apple

Editor: Susan Eddy

Good Apple
An Imprint of Modern Curriculum
A Division of Simon & Schuster
299 Jefferson Road, P.O. Box 480
Parsippany, NJ 07054-0480

ISBN 1–56417–843–9

1 2 3 4 5 6 7 8 9   MAL   01 00 99 98 97 96

CONTENTS

A Word About *Spelling DoodleLoops*

Directions for Teachers

What Are *Spelling DoodleLoops?*

The activities in *Spelling DoodleLoops* are unique learning tools that offer meaningful and stimulating ways to introduce or practice word families—words with similiar sounds and letter patterns. Writing and reading about such words is an effective way to teach spelling skills to beginning readers.

Spelling DoodleLoops introduces 45 different word families. Each family is presented on two consecutive pages. On the first, chlldren fill in letters to complete all the words in the family. Then they identify pictures by correctly spelling the word that describes each picture.

On the second page, children follow a series of directions and complete drawings based on those directions. One or more of the words in the word family is included in each sentence of the directions. For example, if the children are learning or practicing words in the *ad* family, the directions may read:

Fill in the missing letters.
You can find them in the house.
Then draw us.

1. I am a d ___ ___ .

2. I am with my kids, T ___ ___

and Br ___ ___ .

3. T ___ ___ is s ___ ___ .

4. Br ___ ___ is m ___ ___ .

5. I h ___ ___ a b ___ ___ day.

THE
ad
FAMILY

bad	glad	pad
Brad	had	sad
dad	lad	Tad
fad	mad	

How to Use *Spelling DoodleLoops*

Try to spend at least two days on each word family included in *Spelling DoodleLoops*. Introduce word families by distributing copies of the first word family activity to children—the page with the word family house in the center. You may wish to illustrate this page on the chalkboard or display it using an overhead projector.

DOODLE LOOPS

- Introduce the name of the word family and discuss the sounds of the letters. For example, if you are introducing the *ad* family, explain that each word in this family is spelled with an *a-d* at the end. The *a* has a short *a* sound.

- Tell children that the beginning letter (or letters) of each word is written on the house. They are to add the letters *a* and *d* to complete each word. Invite children fo fill in the words in the house. For example: ▶

- Encourage children to take turns reading the words they have made. As each child reads the words, fill them in on the chalkboard or overhead.

- Have children think of other words that end with the same letters. List these words on the chalkboard or overhead as well.

- Direct children's attention to the pictures surrounding the word family house. Ask children to find the word in the house that best describes each picture. Encourage children to spell the words correctly in the spaces provided next to each picture. Help children choose the correct words for each picture the first time they tackle a word family by working with them on the chalkboard or overhead. For example: ▶

5

- After the first word family activity has been completed, distribute copies of the second activity for the same word family. This may be done immediately after completing the first activity or on the following day. You may wish to illustrate this page on the chalkboard or display it using an overhead projector.

- Draw children's attention to the words in the house. Point out that they are the same words that children completed in the large word family house. Tell children that some of these words are found in the sentence at the top of the page.

- Read the directions at the top of the page or invite one of the children to read them. The directions read *Fill in the missing letters. You can find them in the house. Then follow the directions.* The first time children do this page, it may be helpful to read each sentence with them and guide them by filling in the missing letters on the chalkboard or transparency.

- Then ask children to follow the directions to create their illustrations. Emphasize the importance of reading *all* the directions before illustrating. It helps even more to read directions at least twice before starting to draw. Be sure to promote creativity by encouraging children to use vivid colors, create detailed illustrations, and use their imaginations.

- As children continue to work on word families, encourage them to follow the directions on their own.

It is important for children to have a vehicle for sharing their *Spelling DoodleLoops* to reinforce their divergent ideas and enable them to receive support and feedback from their classmates. It is particularly meaningful to share the second activity—the page with the children's own artwork. Children may share their work in a variety of ways—individually or in groups, on bulletin boards, by completing transparencies, or by inviting another class in for sharing.

DoodleLoops may be used as a cooperative learning tool by encouraging two or three children to work on a *DoodleLoop* together. Children will reinforce and teach each other in such a situation. As an assessment tool, you will find that *Spelling DoodleLoops* give a good indication of the development of children's spelling and phonetic skills, comprehension skills, and ability to follow directions.

Family involvement

You may first wish to send home a letter to parents when *Spelling DoodleLoops* are first introduced. A sample letter is provided on page 7. Encourage children to share their *DoodleLoops* with their families. *DoodleLoops* provide a wonderful home-school connection, and families will enjoy sharing their children's progress over the year.

Most of all, enjoy the activities. *DoodleLoops* offer endless possibilities for learning and for expanding creative awareness.

Dear Family,

This year your child will be working on some special activities called *Spelling DoodleLoops*. *Spelling DoodleLoops* offer children an enjoyable way to learn, practice, and reinforce spelling skills. They also serve as an excellent tool for practicing reading skills, following directions, and improving reading comprehension.

Spelling DoodleLoops introduce various word families—words that rhyme and have the same phonetic patterns. Each word family is presented in two consecutive activities. In the first, children fill in letters to complete all the words in the family and then identify pictures. The second provides a short description of a character or scene that children illustrate. Various words from the word family are included in the directions. For example, the two activities illustrated here deal with the word family *ad*.

Please take the time to share and discuss these activities with your child. Thank you for your involvement.

Sincerely,

DoodlE LOOPS

Directions for Parents

Spelling DoodleLoops are a stimulating and enjoyable way to present educational materials to your children. Watch them have fun learning letter sounds, spelling patterns, reading skills, and direction following in a meaningful and exciting fashion.

It is important that you provide some guidance as children tackle *Spelling DoodleLoops*, so each activity becomes a valuable and enriching learning experience. Your involvement and support will also make these activities more meaningful for your children. By encouraging them to read, write, spell, create, and experience the true excitement connected with learning, you share in the fun!

Read the "Directions for Teachers" on pages 4–6 before helping your children begin *Spelling DoodleLoops*. You may wish to illustrate examples on separate sheets of paper rather than on the chalkboard or overhead projector used in the classroom.

Be sure your children share their work with you, other family members, or friends. Display their work! Sharing helps reinforce their ideas and provides an opportunity for support and feedback. Encourage your children to do their best work—to make neat, detailed illustrations and to use their imaginations. Remind them to take their time. This helps children to develop a sense of pride in their finished products. Racing through the *DoodleLoops* book reduces the value of the learning experience. Explore the art of language with your children. You will see their skills and confidence grow as they complete each *DoodleLoops* activity.

DOODLE LOOPS

Fill in the missing letters in the *ad* family.

Then label the pictures.

Br __ __ is gl __ __

THE ad FAMILY

b __ __	l __ __
Br __ __	m __ __
d __ __	p __ __
f __ __	s __ __
gl __ __	T __ __
h __ __	

D __ __ is s __ __   T __ __ is m __ __

9

DOODLE LOOPS

Fill in the missing letters.

You can find them in the house.

Then draw us.

THE ad FAMILY

DOODLE LOOPS

bad	glad	pad
Brad	had	sad
dad	lad	Tad
fad	mad	

1. I am a d ___ ___ .

2. I am with my kids, T ___ ___

and Br ___ ___ .

3. T ___ ___ is s ___ ___ .

4. Br ___ ___ is m ___ ___ .

5. I h ___ ___ a b ___ ___ day!

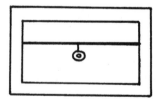

Home Sweet Home

10

DOODLE LOOPS

Fill in the missing letters in the *an* family.

Then label the pictures.

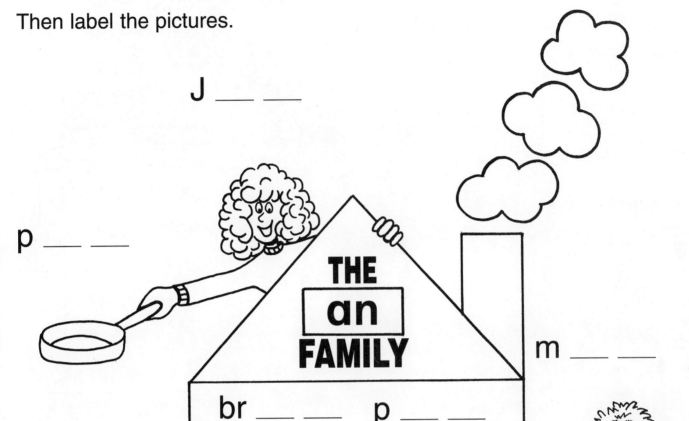

J __ __

p __ __ __

THE **an** FAMILY

br __ __	p __ __
c __ __ __	r __ __ __
D __ __	St __ __ __
f __ __ __	t __ __ __
J __ __ __	th __ __ __
m __ __	v __ __ __
N __ __	

m __ __ __

f __ __

c __ __ __

11

DOODLE LOOPS

Fill in the missing letters.

You can find them in the house.

Then draw us.

THE
an
FAMILY

DOODLE LOOPS

bran	Jan	Stan
can	man	tan
Dan	Nan	than
fan	pan	van
Fran	ran	

1. I am a m ___ ___ .

2. My name is St ___ ___ .

3. I am in a v ___ ___ .

4. The v ___ ___ is t ___ ___ .

5. I see my friends D ___ ___

and Fr___ ___ .

DOODLE LOOPS

Fill in the missing letters in the *at* family.

Then label the pictures.

b __ __

THE at FAMILY

h __ __

b __ __	m __ __
br __ __	P __ __
c __ __	r __ __
ch __ __	s __ __
f __ __	sc __ __
fl __ __	th __ __
h __ __	v __ __

c __ __

WELCOME

P __ __

m __ __

DOODLE LOOPS

Fill in the missing letters.

You can find them in the house.

Then draw me.

THE at FAMILY

DOODLE LOOPS

bat	flat	sat
brat	hat	scat
cat	mat	that
chat	Pat	vat
fat	rat	

1. My name is P___ ___ .

2. I am a f___ ___   c___ ___ .

3. I have a b___ ___ .

4. I s___ ___   on a m___ ___ .

5. I am wearing a funny h___ ___ .

DOODLE LOOPS

Fill in the missing letters in the *ack* family.

Then label the pictures.

t __ __ __

cr __ __ __ __

THE
ack
FAMILY

b __ __ __ __   qu __ __ __ __

bl __ __ __ __   s __ __ __ __

cr __ __ __ __   sh __ __ __ __

J __ __ __ __   sn __ __ __ __

l __ __ __ __   st __ __ __ __

M __ __ __ __   t __ __ __ __

p __ __ __ __   Z __ __ __ __

b __ __ __ __

qu __ __ __ __

s __ __ __ __

Fill in the missing letters.

You can find them in the house.

Then draw us.

1. I am J ___ ___ ___ .

2. I have a b ___ ___ ___

p ___ ___ ___ .

3. My hair is bl ___ ___ ___ .

4. I am eating a sn ___ ___ ___ .

5. I am with my twin M ___ ___ ___ .

THE ack FAMILY

back	Mack	shack
black	pack	snack
crack	quack	stack
Jack	rack	tack
lack	sack	Zack

DoodlE LOOPS

Fill in the missing letters in the *and* family.

Then label the pictures.

s ' __ __ __

THE and FAMILY

b __ __ __ __   h __ __ __ __

bl __ __ __   l __ __ __

br __ __ __ __   s __ __ __ __

gl __ __ __   st __ __ __ __

gr __ __ __ __   str __ __ __ __

h __ __ __ __

headst __ __ __ __

DOODLE LOOPS

Fill in the missing letters.
You can find them in the house.
Then draw us.

THE and FAMILY

1. I am in a rock b ___ ___ ___ .

2. I play the baby gr ___ ___ ___ .

3. Our b ___ ___ ___ is the best in the land.

4. We st ___ ___ ___ in front of our fans .

5. They give us a big h ___ ___ ___ !

band	gland	sand
bland	grand	stand
brand	hand	strand
	land	

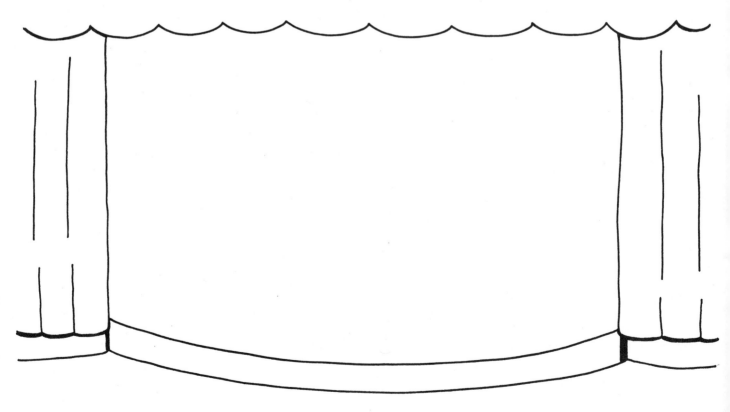

DOODLE LOOPS

Fill in the missing letters in the *ed* family.

Then label the pictures.

sh __ __

THE
ed
FAMILY

b __ __	r __ __ __
bl __ __ __	sh __ __
f __ __ __	sl __ __
J __ __	T __ __
l __ __	w __ __ __
N __ __	

b __ __

w __ __

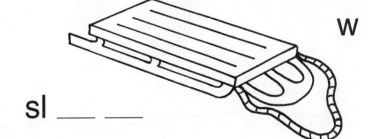

sl __ __

DOODLE LOOPS

Fill in the missing letters.

You can find them in the house.

Then draw us.

THE ed FAMILY

DOODLE LOOPS

bed	led	sled
bled	Ned	Ted
fed	red	wed
Jed	shed	

1. I am T ___ ___ .

2. I am on my sl ___ ___ .

3. I am with J ___ ___ .

4. We are by the sh ___ ___ .

5. Our faces are r ___ ___ .

DOODLE LOOPS

Fill in the missing letters in the *en* family.

Then label the pictures.

10

t _ _

Cluck!

THE **en** FAMILY

B _ _ _	m _ _ _
d _ _ _	p _ _ _
h _ _ _	t _ _ _
J _ _ _	th _ _ _
K _ _ _	wh _ _ _
L _ _ _	wr _ _ _

h _ _ _

p _ _ _

m _ _ _

DOODLE LOOPS

Fill in the missing letters.

You can find them in the house.

Then draw us and our pet.

1. I am L ___ ___ .

2. I have a wife named

   J ___ ___ .

3. My son, K ___ ___ ,

   is t ___ ___ .

4. We are in the d ___ ___ .

5. We have a pet h ___ ___

   named B ___ ___ .

THE en FAMILY

Ben	Ken	ten
den	Len	then
hen	men	when
Jen	pen	wren

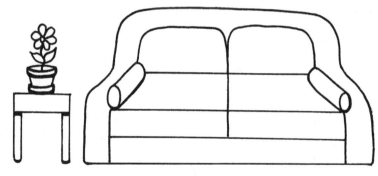

Doodle Loops

Fill in the missing letters in the *et* family.

Then label the pictures.

THE
et
FAMILY

j __ __

b __ __   n __ __
g __ __   p __ __
fr __ __   s __ __
j __ __   v __ __
l __ __   w __ __
m __ __

n __ __

w __ __

p __ __

23

DOODLE LOOPS

Fill in the missing letters.

You can find them in the house.

Then draw me and my pet.

THE
et
FAMILY

bet	let	set
get	met	vet
fret	net	wet
jet	pet	

1. I am a v ___ ___ .

2. I want a new p ___ ___ .

3. I went to a pond to g ___ ___

my p ___ ___ .

4. I caught him in my n ___ ___ .

5. My p ___ ___ is all w ___ ___ .

DOODLE LOOPS

Fill in the missing letters in the *ell* family.

Then label the pictures.

sm __ __ __

sh __ __ __

THE
ell
FAMILY

b __ __ __   sh __ __ __

d __ __ __   sm __ __ __

f __ __ __   sw __ __ __

N __ __ __   t __ __ __

s __ __ __   w __ __ __

b __ __ __   w __ __ __

DOODLE LOOPS

Fill in the missing letters.

You can find them in the house.

Then draw me.

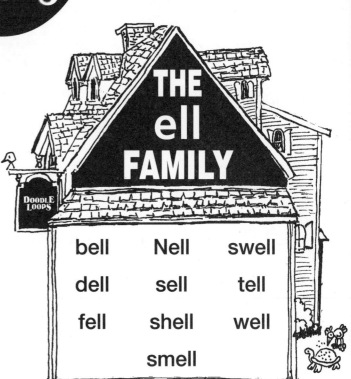

THE ell FAMILY

bell	Nell	swell
dell	sell	tell
fell	shell	well
	smell	

1. I am N ___ ___ ___ .

2. I just f ___ ___ ___ .

3. I don't feel w ___ ___ ___ .

4. My foot is starting to

sw ___ ___ ___ .

5. Don't t ___ ___ ___ my mom!

Fill in the missing letters in the *ig* family.

Then label the pictures.

w ___ ___

THE
ig
FAMILY

b ___ ___   p ___ ___

d ___ ___   r ___ ___

f ___ ___   tw ___ ___

j ___ ___   w ___ ___

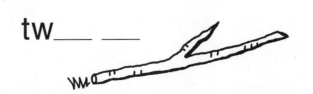

p ___ ___   tw ___ ___   j ___ ___

Fill in the missing letters.
You can find them in the house.
Then draw me.

1. I am a p ___ ___ .

2. I am very b ___ ___ .

3. I am wearing a w ___ ___ .

4. I am doing a j ___ ___ .

5. I am eating a f ___ ___ .

THE ig FAMILY

big	jig	twig
dig	pig	wig
fig	rig	

DOODLE LOOPS

Fill in the missing letters in the *ick* family.

Then label the pictures.

l ___ ___ ___

THE ick FAMILY

br ___ ___ ___	qu ___ ___ ___
ch ___ ___ ___	R ___ ___ ___
cl ___ ___ ___	s ___ ___ ___
D ___ ___ ___	sl ___ ___ ___
k ___ ___ ___	st ___ ___ ___
l ___ ___ ___	t ___ ___ ___
M ___ ___ ___	th ___ ___ ___
N ___ ___ ___	w ___ ___ ___
p ___ ___ ___	

Peep!

ch ___ ___ ___

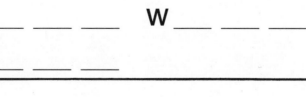

s ___ ___ ___

st ___ ___ ___

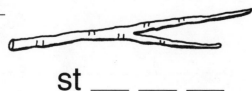

DOODLE LOOPS

Fill in the missing letters.
You can find them in the house.
Then draw Nick, Dick, and Rick.

THE
ick
FAMILY

brick	Mick	slick
chick	Nick	stick
click	pick	thick
Dick	quick	tick
kick	Rick	wick
lick	sick	

1. N ___ ___ ___ plays football.

2. He will k ___ ___ ___ the ball.

3. He kicks it to D ___ ___ ___ .

4. D ___ ___ ___ passes to R ___ ___ ___ .

5. R ___ ___ ___ is qu ___ ___ ___ !

DOODLE LOOPS

Fill in the missing letters in the *ill* family.

Then label the pictures.

h _____ _____ _____

dr _____ _____ _____

THE ill FAMILY

B _____ _____ _____	J _____ _____ _____
ch _____ _____ _____	k _____ _____ _____
d _____ _____ _____	m _____ _____ _____
dr _____ _____ _____	p _____ _____ _____
f _____ _____ _____	qu _____ _____ _____
fr _____ _____ _____	s _____ _____ _____
g _____ _____ _____	sp _____ _____ _____
gr _____ _____ _____	st _____ _____ _____
h _____ _____ _____	w _____ _____ _____

Oops!

gr _____ _____ _____

sp _____ _____ _____

DOODLE LOOPS

Fill in the missing letters.

You can find them in the house.

Then draw me and Jill.

THE ill FAMILY

Bill	gill	pill
chill	grill	quill
dill	hill	sill
drill	ill	spill
fill	Jill	still
frill	kill	will
	mill	

1. I am B ___ ___ ___ .

2. I am feeling ___ ___ ___ .

3. I have a ch ___ ___ ___ .

4. J ___ ___ ___ is giving

me a p ___ ___ ___ .

5. I w ___ ___ ___ lie

st ___ ___ ___ .

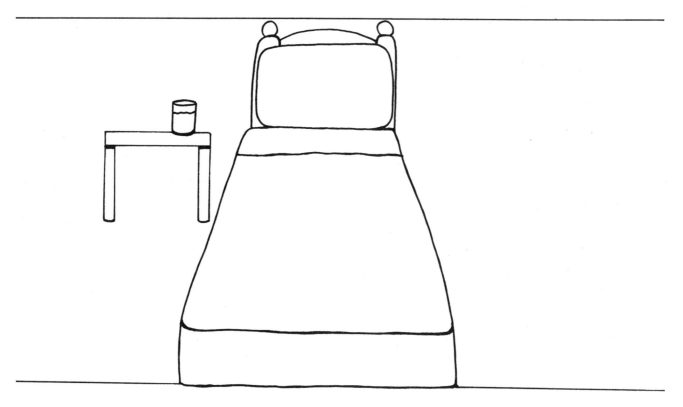

DOODLE LOOPS

Fill in the missing letters in the *ing* family.

Then label the pictures.

w _____ _____ _____

THE
ing
FAMILY

s _____ _____ _____

br _____ _____ _____	s _____ _____ _____
cl _____ _____ _____	sl _____ _____ _____
fl _____ _____ _____	str _____ _____ _____
k _____ _____ _____	th _____ _____ _____
r _____ _____ _____	w _____ _____ _____

La, la, la, la

k _____ _____ _____

r _____ _____ _____

33

Doodle Loops

THE ing FAMILY

Fill in the missing letters.

You can find them in the house.

Then draw me.

1. I am a Th ___ ___ ___ .

2. I have one w ___ ___ ___ .

3. I wear a r ___ ___ ___ .

4. I am the K ___ ___ ___

of all Things .

5. I love to s ___ ___ ___ .

bring	King	string
cling	ring	Thing
fling	sing	wing
	sling	

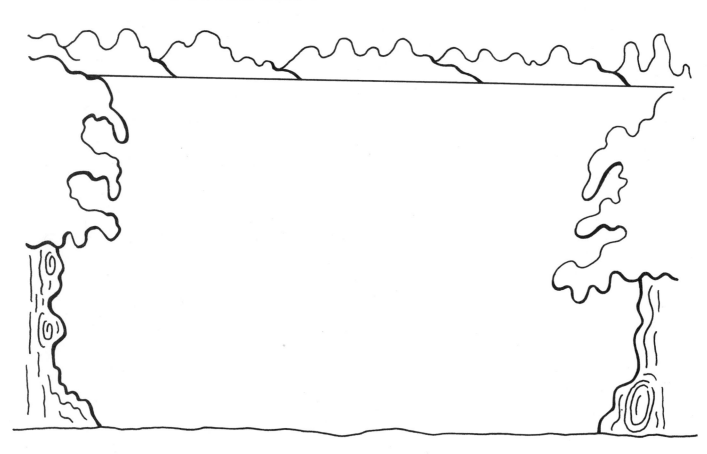

DOODLE LOOPS

Fill in the missing letters in the *ot* family.

Then label the pictures.

p _ _ _

THE ot FAMILY

kn _ _ _

bl _ _	n _ _ _
cl _ _ _	pl _ _
c _ _ _	p _ _ _
d _ _ _	r _ _ _
g _ _ _	sh _ _
h _ _ _	sl _ _
j _ _ _	sp _ _ _
kn _ _ _	t _ _ _
l _ _ _	tr _ _ _

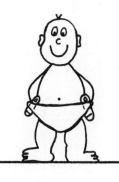

h _ _ _

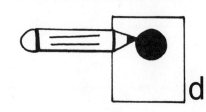

d _ _ _ _

t _ _ _

35

DOODLE LOOPS

Fill in the missing letters.

You can find them in the house.

Then draw us.

1. I am a t ___ ___ .

2. I am very h___ ___ .

3. I am on a c ___ ___ .

4. I am getting a sh ___ ___ .

5. I g ___ ___ the chicken pox.

THE ot FAMILY

blot	jot	rot
clot	knot	shot
cot	lot	slot
dot	not	spot
got	plot	tot
hot	pot	trot

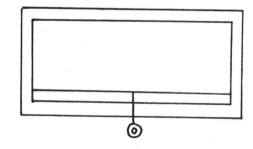

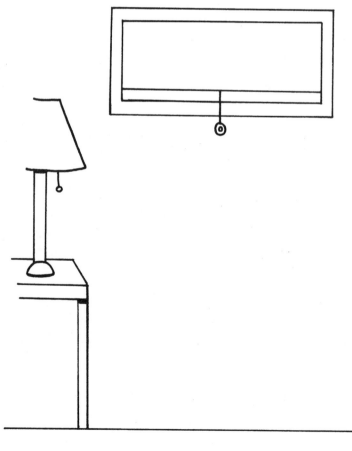

DoodlE LOOPS

Fill in the missing letters in the *un* family.

Then label the pictures.

s _ _ _

THE
un
FAMILY

beg _ _ _	p _ _ _
b _ _ _	r _ _ _
f _ _ _	sh _ _ _
g _ _ _	st _ _ _
n _ _ _	s _ _ _

Yum!

r _ _ _

b _ _ _

DOODLE LOOPS

Fill in the missing letters.
You can find them in the house.
Then draw me.

1. I am having f ___ ___ .

2. I have a squirt g ___ ___ .

3. I r ___ ___ and r ___ ___ .

4. I am lying in the s ___ ___ .

5. I am eating a hot dog

on a b ___ ___ .

THE
un
FAMILY

begun	gun	shun
bun	nun	stun
fun	pun	sun
	run	

DOODLE LOOPS

Fill in the missing letters in the *ump* family.

Then label the pictures.

j _____ _____ _____

THE ump **FAMILY**

b _____ _____ _____

h _____ _____ _____ _____

b _____ _____ _____   l _____ _____ _____

cl _____ _____ _____   pl _____ _____ _____

d _____ _____ _____   p _____ _____ _____

gr _____ _____ _____   sl _____ _____ _____

h _____ _____ _____   st _____ _____ _____

j _____ _____ _____   th _____ _____ _____

st _____ _____ _____

DOODLE LOOPS

Fill in the missing letters.

You can find them in the house.

Then draw me.

THE ump FAMILY

bump	hump	pump
clump	jump	slump
dump	lump	stump
grump	plump	thump

1. I am a gr ___ ___ ___ .

2. I am very pl ___ ___ ___ .

3. I like to j ___ ___ ___ .

4. I j ___ ___ ___ from

st ___ ___ ___ to st ___ ___ ___ .

5. I land with a th ___ ___ ___ .

DOODLE LOOPS

Fill in the missing letters in the *ace* family.

Then label the pictures.

      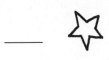

sp _____ _____ _____

THE

ace

FAMILY

br_____ _____ _____   pl_____ _____ _____

f_____ _____ _____ _____   r_____ _____ _____

Gr_____ _____ _____   sp_____ _____ _____

l_____ _____ _____   tr_____ _____ _____

p_____ _____ _____

f _____ _____ _____

Gr _____ _____ _____

l _____ _____ _____

DOODLE LOOPS

Fill in the missing letters.
You can find them in the house.
Then draw us.

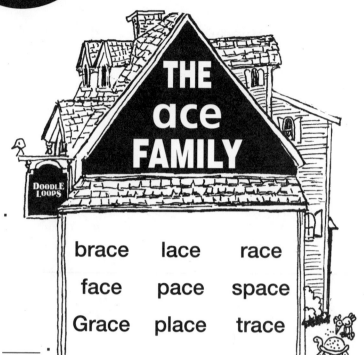

THE ace FAMILY

DOODLE LOOPS

brace	lace	race
face	pace	space
Grace	place	trace

1. I am in a r___ ___ ___ .

2. I am in first pl ___ ___ ___ .

3. I have a smile on

my f ___ ___ ___ .

4. I am from outer sp ___ ___ ___ .

Finish

DOODLE LOOPS

Fill in the missing letters in the *ake* family.

Then label the pictures.

THE  **ake FAMILY**

l _ _ _

b _ _ _	qu _ _ _
br _ _ _	r _ _ _
c _ _ _	s _ _ _
dr _ _ _	sh _ _ _
f _ _ _	sn _ _ _
fl _ _ _	st _ _ _
J _ _ _	t _ _ _
l _ _ _	w _ _ _
m _ _ _	

r _ _ _

c _ _ _

sn _ _ _

DOODLE LOOPS

Fill in the missing letters.

You can find them in the house.

Then draw us.

THE ake FAMILY

bake	Jake	shake
brake	lake	snake
cake	make	stake
drake	quake	take
fake	rake	wake
flake	sake	

1. My name is J ___ ___ ___ .

2. I am with my pet

sn ___ ___ ___ .

3. We both like to b ___ ___ ___ .

4. We just made a c ___ ___ ___ .

5. We are eating it by a

l ___ ___ ___ .

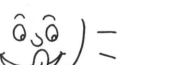

44

DOODLE LOOPS

Fill in the missing letters in the *ame* family.

Then label the pictures.

THE
ame
FAMILY

t _ _ _ _

n _ _ _ _ _

Hi!
I am
James

bl_ _ _ _   M_ _ _ _

c_ _ _ _   n_ _ _ _

d_ _ _ _   s_ _ _ _

f_ _ _ _   sh_ _ _ _

g_ _ _ _   t_ _ _ _

l_ _ _ _

s _ _ _ _

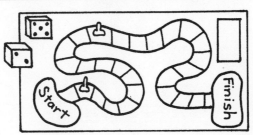

g _ _ _ _

DOODLE LOOPS

Fill in the missing letters.
You can find them in the house.
Then draw us.

1. I am playing a g ___ ___ ___ .

2. My brother c ___ ___ ___ in.

3. We look the s ___ ___ ___ .

4. We have the s ___ ___ ___

last n ___ ___ ___ .

5. But my first n ___ ___ ___

is M ___ ___ ___ .

THE
ame
FAMILY

blame	game	same
came	lame	shame
dame	Mame	tame
fame	name	

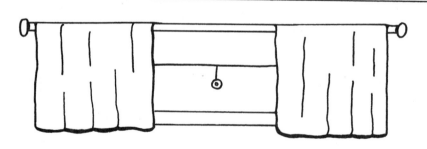

DOODLE LOOPS

Fill in the missing letters in the *ane* family.

Then label the pictures.

pl _ _ _

THE
ane
FAMILY

J _ _ _ _

c _ _ _ _   m _ _ _

cr _ _ _ _   pl _ _ _

d _ _ _ _   s _ _ _

J _ _ _ _   v _ _ _

l _ _ _

m _ _ _   c _ _ _ _

47

DOODLE LOOPS

Fill in the missing letters.

You can find them in the house.

Then draw us.

THE
ane
FAMILY

DOODLE
LOOPS

1. I am J ___ ___ ___ .

2. I use a c ___ ___ ___ .

3. I have a Great D ___ ___ ___ .

cane	Jane	plane
crane	lane	sane
Dane	mane	vane

4. We walk down

the l ___ ___ ___ .

5. We can see a jet

pl ___ ___ ___ .

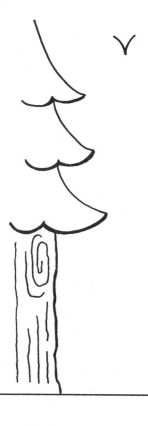

DOODLE LOOPS

Fill in the missing letters in the *ate* family.

Then label the pictures.

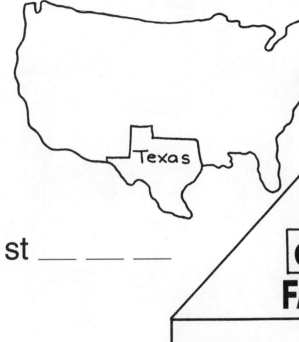

Texas

st ___ ___ ___

THE
ate
FAMILY

d___ ___ ___   N___ ___ ___

f___ ___ ___   pl___ ___ ___

g___ ___ ___   r___ ___ ___

h___ ___ ___   sl___ ___ ___

K___ ___ ___   sk___ ___ ___

l___ ___ ___   st___ ___ ___

pl ___ ___ ___

g ___ ___ ___

sk ___ ___ ___ ___

Fill in the missing letters.

You can find them in the house.

Then draw us.

THE ate FAMILY

ate	hate	rate
date	Kate	skate
fate	late	slate
gate	Nate	state
	plate	

1. My name is N ___ ___ ___ .

2. I have a d ___ ___ ___ .

3. Her name is K ___ ___ ___ .

4. First we ___ ___ ___ .

5. Now we are going

to sk ___ ___ ___ .

Thin Ice!

DOODLE LOOPS

Fill in the missing letters in the *ail* family.

Then label the pictures.

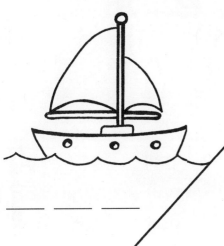

THE
ail
FAMILY

s __ __ __

b __ __ __   p __ __ __ __

f __ __ __   qu __ __ __

G __ __ __ __   r __ __ __

h __ __ __   s __ __ __

j __ __ __   sn __ __ __

m __ __ __   t __ __ __

n __ __ __   tr __ __ __

n __ __ __ __   t __ __ __

sn __ __ __

p __ __ __ __

DOODLE LOOPS

Fill in the missing letters.
You can find them in the house.
Then draw me.

THE
ail
FAMILY

DOODLE
LOOPS

bail	mail	sail
fail	nail	snail
Gail	pail	tail
hail	quail	trail
jail	rail	

1. I am G ___ ___ ___ .

2. I am walking on a

tr ___ ___ ___ .

3. I have a p ___ ___ ___ .

4. I just found a sn ___ ___ ___ .

5. It is starting to h ___ ___ ___ .

DOODLE LOOPS

Fill in the missing letters in the *ain* family.

Then label the pictures.

tr _ _ _

4, 862,347
+1, 976,002
6,838,349

E=MC²

THE ain FAMILY

br_ _ _ _   p_ _ _ _
ch_ _ _ _   pl_ _ _ _
dr_ _ _ _   r_ _ _ _
g_ _ _ _   st_ _ _ _
gr_ _ _ _   str_ _ _ _
m_ _ _ _   tr_ _ _ _

r _ _ _

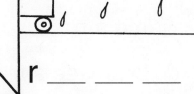

br _ _ _   ch _ _ _

DOODLE LOOPS

Fill in the missing letters.
You can find them in the house.
Then draw me.

THE ain FAMILY

brain	grain	rain
chain	Main	stain
drain	pain	strain
gain	plain	train

1. I am in the r ___ ___ ___ .

2. I am on M ___ ___ ___

Street .

3. I am wearing a ch ___ ___ ___ .

4. The ch ___ ___ ___ gives

me a p ___ ___ ___ .

5. I can see a tr ___ ___ ___ .

Main Street

DOODLE LOOPS

Fill in the missing letters in the *ay* family.

Then label the pictures.

j __ __

K __ __

spr __ __ __

THE ay FAMILY

aw __ __		m __ __ __	
b __ __		p __ __ __	
cl __ __		pl __ __	
d __ __		pr __ __	
F __ __ __		R __ __ __	
g __ __		s __ __ __	
gr __ __		spr __ __	
h __ __		st __ __	
J __ __		str __ __	
K __ __		tr __ __	
l __ __		w __ __	

h __ __

tr __ __

DoodlE LOOPS

Fill in the missing letters.
You can find them in the house.
Then draw us.

THE ay FAMILY

DoodlE LOOPS

away	hay	Ray
bay	Jay	say
clay	Kay	spray
day	lay	stay
Fay	may	stray
gay	pay	tray
gray	play	way
	pray	

1. We are F ___ ___

and K ___ ___ .

2. We like to pl ___ ___ .

3. We pl ___ ___ with cl ___ ___ .

4. The cl ___ ___ is on

a tr ___ ___ .

5. The cl ___ ___ is gr ___ ___ .

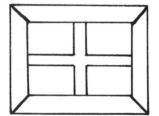
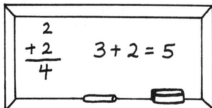
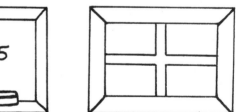

3 + 2 = 5

DOODLE LOOPS

Fill in the missing letters in the *ear* family.

Then label the pictures.

t _____ _____ _____

THE
ear
FAMILY

sp _____ _____ _____

cl_____ _____ _____   r_____ _____ _____

d_____ _____ _____   sh_____ _____ _____

f_____ _____ _____   sp_____ _____ _____

g_____ _____ _____   t_____ _____ _____

h_____ _____ _____   y_____ _____ _____

n _____ _____ _____

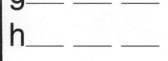

f _____ _____ _____

CALENDAR

1996

y _____ _____ _____

57

DOODLE LOOPS

Fill in the missing letters.

You can find them in the house.

Then draw me.

1. The day is cl ___ ___ ___ .

2. I h ___ ___ ___ a sound .

3. It is danger, I f ___ ___ ___ .

4. It is coming n ___ ___ ___ .

5. I grab my sp ___ ___ ___ .

THE ear FAMILY

clear	hear	spear
dear	near	tear
fear	rear	year
gear	shear	

DOODLE LOOPS

Fill in the missing letters in the *eat* family.

Then label the pictures.

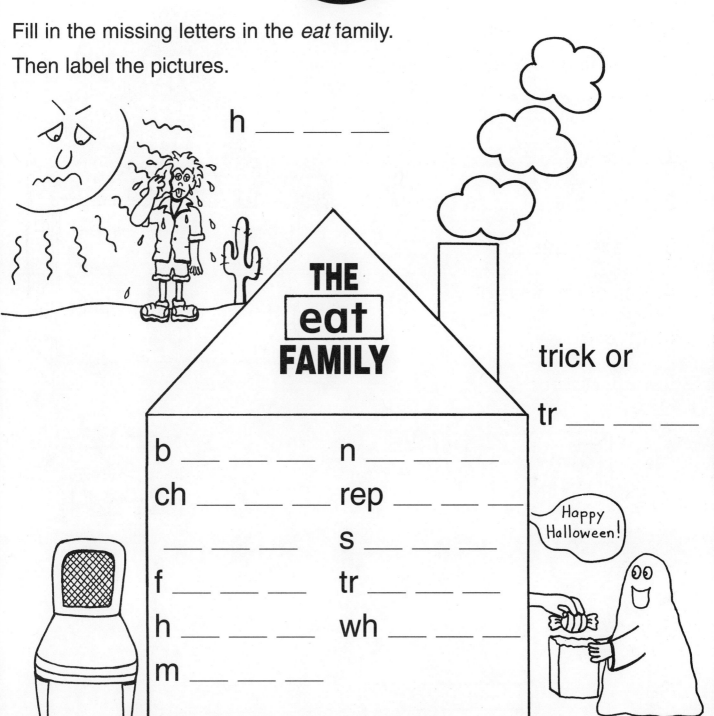

h _____ _____ _____

trick or

tr _____ _____ _____ _____

THE
eat
FAMILY

b _____ _____ _____   n _____ _____ _____

ch _____ _____ _____   rep _____ _____ _____

_____ _____ _____   s _____ _____ _____

f _____ _____ _____   tr _____ _____ _____

h _____ _____ _____   wh _____ _____ _____

m _____ _____ _____

Happy Halloween!

s _____ _____ _____ _____

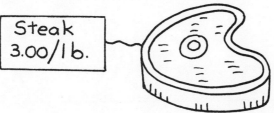

Steak 3.00/lb.

m _____ _____ _____ _____

DOODLE LOOPS

Fill in the missing letters.
You can find them in the house.
Then draw me.

THE eat FAMILY

beat	heat	seat
cheat	meat	treat
eat	neat	wheat
feat	repeat	

1. I like to ___ ___ ___ .

2. I take a s ___ ___ ___ .

3. I am having a tr ___ ___ ___ .

4. It is some kind of

m ___ ___ ___ .

5. I am not n ___ ___ ___ .

My Kitchen

DOODLE LOOPS

Fill in the missing letters in the *eed* family.

Then label the pictures.

W __ __ __

THE
eed
FAMILY

Ouch!

Mmmm!

bl __ __ __   ind __ __ __   bl __ __ __

br __ __ __ __   n __ __ __

d __ __ __ __   s __ __ __

f __ __ __ __   sp __ __ __

gr __ __ __ __   w __ __ __

h __ __ __

f __ __ __

s __ __ __ __

DOODLE LOOPS

Fill in the missing letters.

You can find them in the house.

Then draw my plant and me.

THE eed FAMILY

bleed	greed	seed
breed	heed	speed
deed	indeed	weed
feed	need	

1. I plant a s __ __ __ .

2. I f __ __ __ my

s __ __ __ .

3. Then I w __ __ __ .

4. It grows so big, ind __ __ __ !

5. What a strange br __ __ __ !

Doodle Loops

Fill in the missing letters in the *eep* family.

Then label the pictures.

w _ _ _ _

THE
eep
FAMILY

sh _ _ _

b _ _ _ _	sh _ _ _
ch _ _ _ _	sl _ _ _
d _ _ _ _	st _ _ _
J _ _ _ _	sw _ _ _
k _ _ _ _	w _ _ _
p _ _ _	

sl _ _ _ _

BAAAA

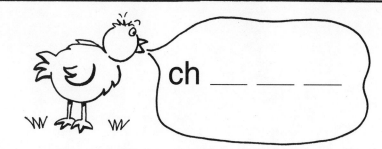

ch _ _ _ _

DoodlE LOOPS

Fill in the missing letters.

You can find them in the house.

Then draw the Jeep and the sheep.

THE eep FAMILY

beep	keep	steep
cheep	peep	sweep
deep	sheep	weep
Jeep	sleep	

1. I see a J ___ ___ ___ .

2. It is full of sh ___ ___ ___ .

3. Some sh ___ ___ ___

sl ___ ___ ___ .

4. Some sh ___ ___ ___

w ___ ___ ___ .

5. The horn goes b ___ ___ ___ .

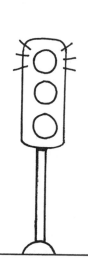

DOODLE LOOPS

Fill in the missing letters in the *eet* family.

Then label the pictures.

tw _ _ _

THE
eet
FAMILY

b _ _ _ _   sh _ _ _ _

f _ _ _   sl _ _ _ _

fl _ _ _   str _ _ _

gr _ _ _ _   sw _ _ _ _

m _ _ _ _   tw _ _ _ _

f _ _ _   m _ _ _

b _ _ _

DOODLE LOOPS

Fill in the missing letters.
You can find them in the house.
Then draw us.

THE
eet
FAMILY

DOODLE LOOPS

beet	greet	street
feet	meet	sweet
fleet	sheet	tweet
	sleet	

1. We walk down the

   str ___ ___ ___ .

2. We m ___ ___ ___ .

3. We gr ___ ___ ___ .

4. We have huge f ___ ___ ___ .

5. We are in the sl ___ ___ ___ .

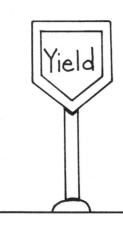

Yield

DOODLE LOOPS

Fill in the missing letters in the *ide* family.

Then label the pictures.

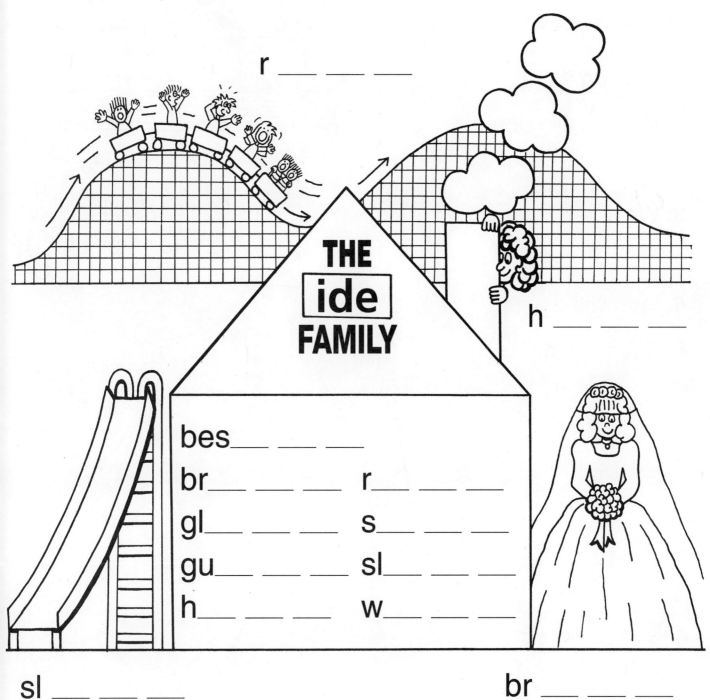

r ___ ___ ___

h ___ ___ ___

THE
ide
FAMILY

bes___ ___ ___

br___ ___ ___   r___ ___ ___

gl___ ___ ___   s___ ___ ___

gu___ ___ ___   sl___ ___ ___

h___ ___ ___   w___ ___ ___

sl ___ ___ ___

br ___ ___ ___

DoodlE LOOPS

Fill in the missing letters.

You can find them in the house.

Then draw me and my bride.

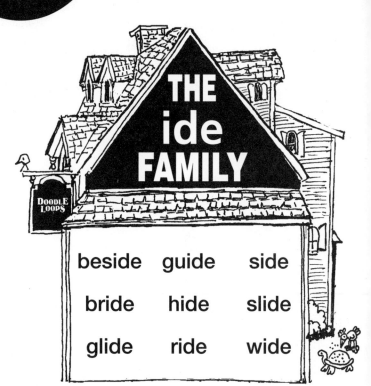

THE ide FAMILY

beside	guide	side
bride	hide	slide
glide	ride	wide

1. I am on a r ___ ___ ___ .

2. I am on a water

sl ___ ___ ___ .

3. We splash and we

gl ___ ___ ___ .

4. I am with my br ___ ___ ___ .

5. She is by my s ___ ___ ___ .

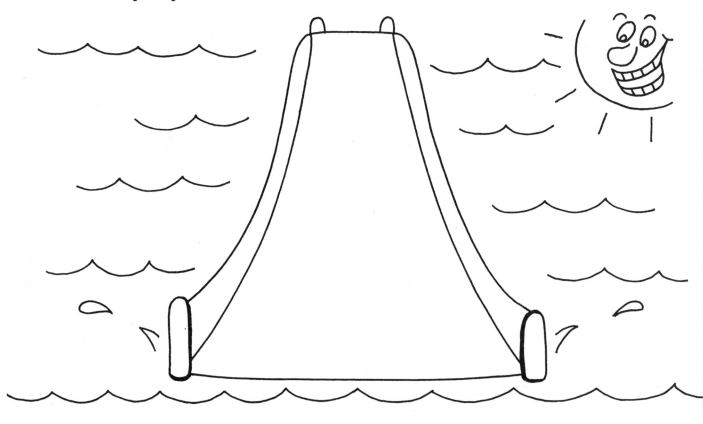

68

Fill in the missing letters in the *ine* family.

Then label the pictures.

l __ __ __

w __ __ __

THE ine FAMILY

d __ __ __   n __ __ __

div __ __ __   p __ __ __

f __ __ __   v __ __ __

l __ __ __   wh __ __ __

m __ __ __   w __ __ __

v __ __ __

n __ __ __

©1996 Sandy Baker   69

DOODLE LOOPS

THE
ine
FAMILY

dine	line	vine
divine	mine	whine
fine	nine	wine
	pine	

Fill in the missing letters.

You can find them in the house.

Then draw us.

1. We d ___ ___ ___ .

2. It is n ___ ___ ___ .

3. We have w ___ ___ ___ .

4. We all sit in a l ___ ___ ___ .

5. Our meal is div ___ ___ ___ .

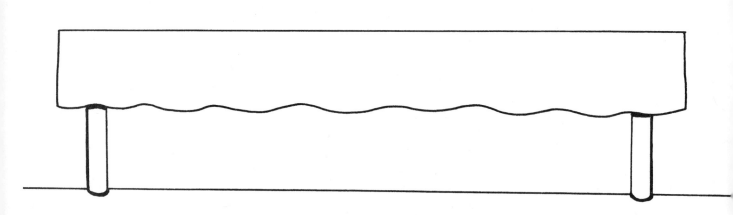

DOODLE LOOPS

Fill in the missing letters in the *ight* family.

Then label the pictures.

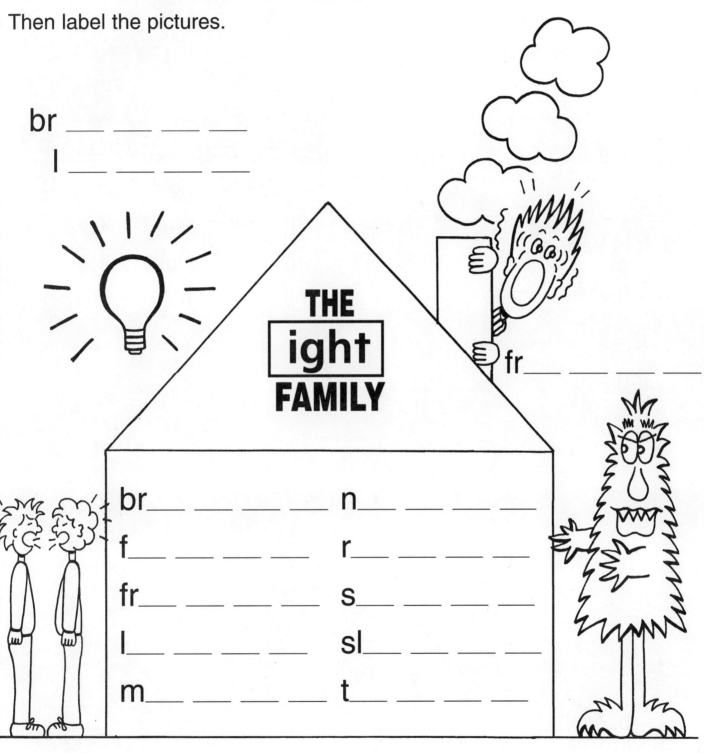

br _____ _____ _____ _____

l _____ _____ _____ _____

THE
ight
FAMILY

fr _____ _____ _____ _____

br _____ _____ _____ _____   n _____ _____ _____ _____

f _____ _____ _____ _____   r _____ _____ _____ _____

fr _____ _____ _____ _____   s _____ _____ _____ _____

l _____ _____ _____ _____   sl _____ _____ _____ _____

m _____ _____ _____ _____   t _____ _____ _____ _____

f _____ _____ _____ _____

Fill in the missing letters.

You can find them in the house.

Then draw the strange sight.

THE ight FAMILY

bright	light	sight
fight	might	slight
fright	night	tight
	right	

1. It is n ___ ___ ___ ___ .

2. I see a strange

s ___ ___ ___ ___ .

3. It is very br ___ ___ ___ ___ .

4. It makes the sky

l ___ ___ ___ ___ .

5. It gives me a fr ___ ___ ___ ___ .

DOODLE LOOPS

Fill in the missing letters in the *ow* family.

Then label the pictures.

scarecr __ __

THE
OW
FAMILY

r __ __

bl __ __	l __ __
b __ __ __	m __ __
cr __ __ __	sh __ __
fl __ __ __	sl __ __ __
gl __ __ __	sn __ __ __
gr __ __ __	r __ __
kn __ __ __	t __

bl __ __ __

b __ __ __

sn __ __

Fill in the missing letters.

You can find them in the house.

Then draw us.

1. We stand in a r ___ ___ .

2. We move very sl ___ ___ .

3. We gr ___ ___ very tired !

4. The moon has a bright

gl ___ ___ .

5. The wind starts to bl ___ ___ .

THE OW FAMILY

blow	grow	show
bow	know	slow
crow	low	snow
flow	mow	tow
glow	row	

DOODLE LOOPS

Fill in the missing letters in the *y* family.

Then label the pictures.

sk ___

THE
y
FAMILY

bu ___   pl ___

b ___   pr ___

cr ___   sh ___

dr ___   sk ___

fl ___   sl ___

fr ___   tr ___

gu ___   wh ___

m ___

fr ___

fl ___

cr ___

DOODLE LOOPS

Fill in the missing letters.
You can find them in the house.
Then draw yourself and the guy
in the sky.

1. I am a gu ___ .

2. I know how to fl ___ .

3. I'm way up in the sk ___ .

4. Wh ___ don't you tr ___ ?

5. Come on! Don't be sh ___ !

THE
y
FAMILY

buy	fry	shy
by	guy	sky
cry	my	sly
dry	ply	try
fly	pry	Why

DOODLE LOOPS

Fill in the missing letters in the *all* family.

Then label the pictures.

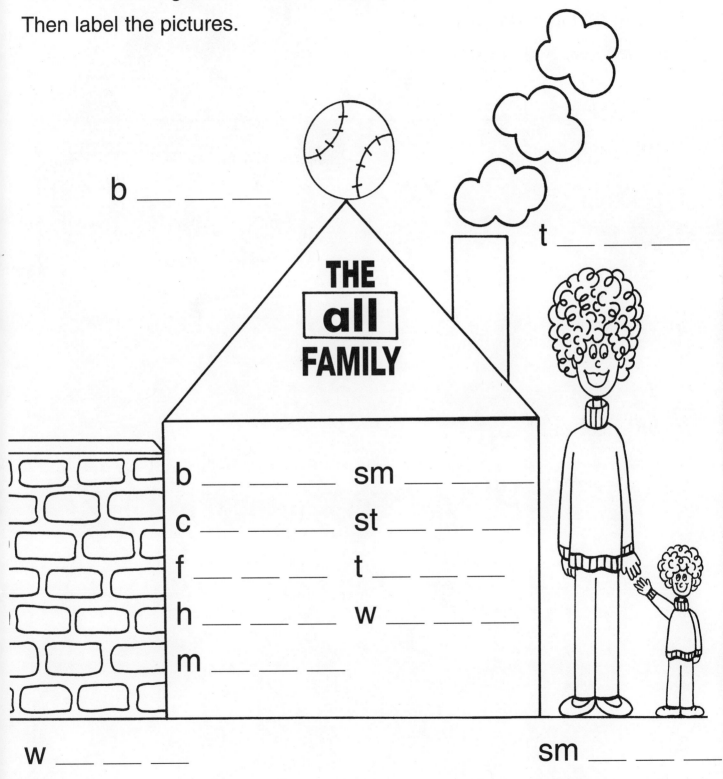

b _ _ _

t _ _ _ _

THE all FAMILY

b _ _ _   sm _ _ _ _
c _ _ _ _   st _ _ _
f _ _ _ _   t _ _ _ _
h _ _ _   w _ _ _
m _ _ _

w _ _ _   sm _ _ _

DOODLE LOOPS

Fill in the missing letters.
You can find them in the house.
Then follow the directions.

THE **all** FAMILY

basketball		stall
call	hall	tall
fall	mall	wall
	small	

1. We are very t ___ ___ ___ .

2. We are playing

basketb ___ ___ ___ .

3. We are playing near

the m ___ ___ ___ .

4. We play against the

w ___ ___ ___ .

5. Did Michael f ___ ___ ___ ?

Who are we? Draw us.

DOODLE LOOPS

Fill in the missing letters in the *ark* family.

Then label the pictures.

sh __ __ __

THE ark FAMILY

p __ __ __

b __ __ __
Cl __ __ __
d __ __ __
h __ __ __
l __ __ __

M __ __ __
p __ __ __
sh __ __ __
sp __ __ __
st __ __ __

Arf!

Mark

b __ __ __

M __ __ __

79

DOODLE LOOPS

Fill in the missing letters.

You can find them in the house.

Then draw us in the park.

THE ark FAMILY

bark	hark	shark
Clark	lark	spark
dark	Mark	stark
	park	

1. I am Cl ___ ___ ___ .

2. I am with M ___ ___ ___ .

3. We walk in the p ___ ___ ___ .

4. My dog starts to b ___ ___ ___ .

5. It is very d ___ ___ ___ .

DOODLE LOOPS

Fill in the missing letters in the *art* family.

Then label the pictures.

d _____ _____ _____

THE
art
FAMILY

p _____ _____ _____

ap_____ _____ _____	m_____ _____ _____
B_____ _____ _____	p_____ _____ _____
c_____ _____ _____	sm_____ _____ _____
ch_____ _____ _____	st_____ _____ _____
d_____ _____ _____	t _____ _____ _____
dep _____ _____ _____	

c _____ _____ _____

B _____ _____ _____

Doodle Loops

THE
art
FAMILY

apart	dart	smart
Bart	depart	start
cart	mart	tart
chart	part	

Fill in the missing letters.
You can find them in the house.
Then draw me at the mart.

1. My name is B ___ ___ ___ .

2. I am at the food

m ___ ___ ___ .

3. I am pushing a c ___ ___ ___ .

4. I just got a t ___ ___ ___ .

5. It is time to dep ___ ___ ___ .

SALE
50¢

SUPER MART
☆ SALE! ☆

82

DOODLE LOOPS

Fill in the missing letters in the *ore* family.

Then label the pictures.

THE **ore** FAMILY

st _ _ _ _

b _ _ _ _   sn _ _ _ _

ch _ _ _ _   s _ _ _ _

c _ _ _ _   st _ _ _ _

m _ _ _ _   t _ _ _ _

sc _ _ _ _   w _ _ _ _

sh _ _ _ _

Oops!

t _ _ _ _

c _ _ _ _

sn _ _ _ _

©1996 Sandy Baker

DoodlE Loops

Fill in the missing letters.
You can find them in the house.
Then draw me by my store.

THE
ore
FAMILY

bore	score	store
chore	shore	tore
core	snore	wore
more	sore	

1. I sit by the sh ___ ___ ___ .

2. There is no one at

my st ___ ___ ___ .

3. This is really a b ___ ___ ___ .

4. I begin to sn ___ ___ ___ .

5. I want to do m ___ ___ ___ .

DOODLE LOOPS

Fill in the missing letters in the *ew* family.

Then label the pictures.

fl __ __

THE **ew** **FAMILY**

bl __ __   gr __ __

br __ __   kn __ __

ch __ __   m __ __

cr __ __   n __ __

d __ __   scr __ __

dr __ __   st __ __

f __ __   vi __ __

fl __ __

m __ __

scr __ __

br __ __

DOODLE LOOPS

Fill in the missing letters.

You can find them in the house.

Then draw the crew, the spaceship,

and the alien plants.

THE ew FAMILY

blew	drew	mew
brew	few	new
chew	flew	screw
crew	grew	stew
dew	knew	view

1. We are a UFO cr ___ ___ .

2. We just fl ___ ___ to Earth.

3. Our spaceship is n ___ ___ .

4. We planted a f ___ ___

  alien seeds.

5. They gr ___ ___ and gr___ ___ .

DOODLE LOOPS

Fill in the missing letters in the *ow* family.

Then label the pictures.

br ___ ___

THE
OW
FAMILY

b ___ ___   n ___ ___

br ___ ___   pl ___ ___

ch ___ ___   p ___ ___

c ___ ___   v ___ ___

h ___ ___   w ___ ___

me ___ ___

me ___ ___

c ___ ___

87

Fill in the missing letters.

You can find them in the house.

Then draw me.

1. I am a c ___ ___ .

2. I don't know h ___ ___ ,

but I say, "Me ___ ___ !"

3. W ___ ___ !

4. Please help me n ___ ___ !

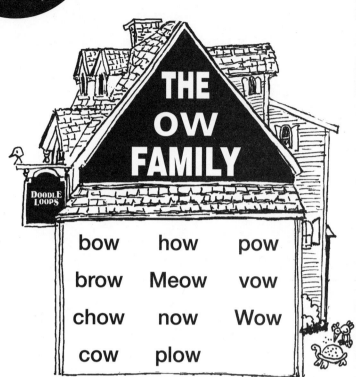

THE OW FAMILY

bow	how	pow
brow	Meow	vow
chow	now	Wow
cow	plow	

DOODLE LOOPS

Fill in the missing letters in the *own* family.

Then label the pictures.

fr _____ _____ _____

cr_____ _____ _____

THE **own** FAMILY

br_____ _____ _____   dr_____ _____ _____

cl_____ _____ _____   fr_____ _____ _____

cr_____ _____ _____   g _____ _____ _____

d_____ _____ _____   t_____ _____ _____

cl _____ _____ _____

g _____ _____ _____

Fill in the missing letters.
You can find them in the house.
Then draw me.

THE
own
FAMILY

brown	down	gown
clown	drown	town
crown	frown	

1. I am a cl ___ ___ ___ .

2. I have a fr___ ___ ___ on

my face .

3. Rain is pouring d ___ ___ ___ .

4. I am wearing a g ___ ___ ___

and a cr ___ ___ ___ .

5. My g ___ ___ ___ is br ___ ___ ___ .

DOODLE LOOPS

Fill in the missing letters in the *ound* family.

Then label the pictures.

ar __ __ __ __

THE
ound
FAMILY

ar __ __ __ __   m __ __ __ __

b __ __ __ __   p __ __ __ __

f __ __ __ __   r __ __ __ __

gr __ __ __ __   s __ __ __ __

h __ __ __ __   w __ __ __ __

gr __ __ __ __   h __ __ __ __

DOODLE LOOPS

Fill in the missing letters.

You can find them in the house.

Then draw me and what I found.

THE
ound

around	mound
bound	pound
found	round
ground	sound
hound	wound

1. I am a h ___ ___ ___ ___ .

2. I am big and

r ___ ___ ___ ___ .

3. I don't make a

s ___ ___ ___ ___ .

4. Look what I f ___ ___ ___ ___ .

5. I hid it in the gr ___ ___ ___ ___ .

DOODLE LOOPS

Fill in the missing letters in the *ook* family.

Then label the pictures.

h _ _ _

THE
ook
FAMILY

b _ _ _   h _ _ _

br _ _ _   l _ _ _

c _ _ _   sh _ _ _

cr _ _ _   t _ _ _

c _ _ _   b _ _ _

Fill in the missing letters.

You can find them in the house.

Then draw me and my book.

Where did I find my book?

THE ook FAMILY

book   crook   shook

brook   hook   took

cook   Look

1. I am a c ___ ___ ___ .

2. I can't find my c ___ ___ ___

b ___ ___ ___ .

3. Who t ___ ___ ___ it ?

4. Was it a cr ___ ___ ___ ?

5. L ___ ___ ___ ! I found

my b ___ ___ ___ !

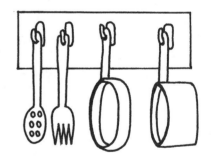

DOODLE LOOPS

Fill in the missing letters in the *oon* family.

Then label the pictures.

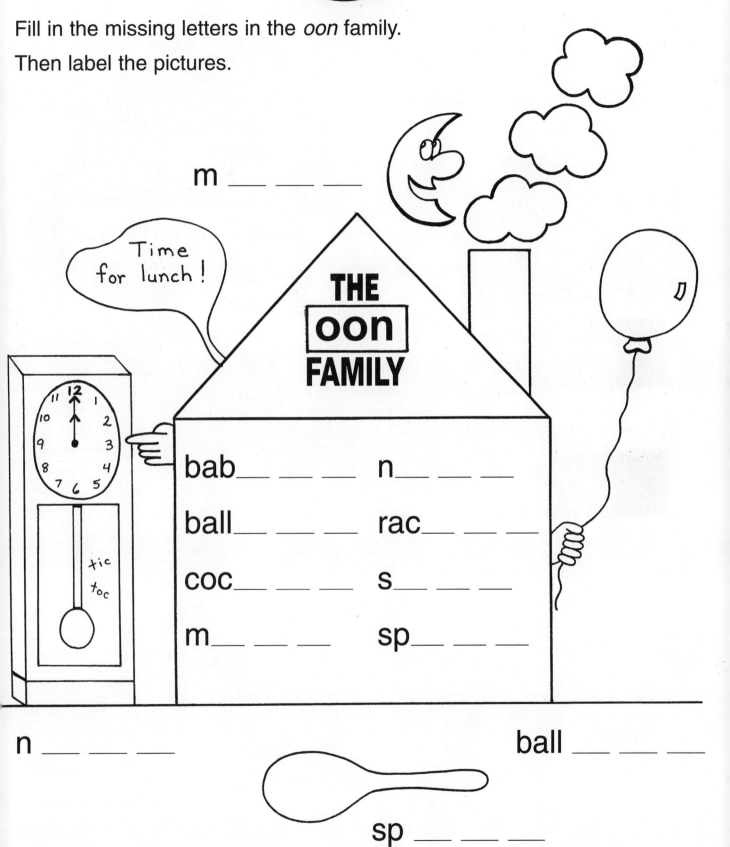

m _ _ _

Time for lunch!

THE
oon
FAMILY

bab_ _ _   n_ _ _

ball_ _ _   rac_ _ _

coc_ _ _   s_ _ _

m_ _ _   sp_ _ _

tic toc

n _ _ _   ball _ _ _

sp _ _ _

DOODLE LOOPS

Fill in the missing letters.
You can find them in the house.
Then draw us and our rocket
on the moon.

THE
oon
FAMILY

baboon	noon
balloon	racoon
cocoon	soon
moon	spoon

1. I am on the m ___ ___ ___ .

2. It is n ___ ___ ___ .

3. I am with a bab ___ ___ ___ .

4. We each have a

ball ___ ___ ___ .

5. We will get in our rocket s ___ ___ ___ .